# THE GOING UNDER OF THE EVENING LAND

# THE GOING UNDER
# OF THE EVENING LAND

poems by

Mekeel McBride

**Carnegie-Mellon University Press**
**Pittsburgh 1983**
Feffer and Simons, Inc., London

# ACKNOWLEDGEMENTS

*Aspect*: "The Pharmacist Goes Cloud Bathing"; *Aspen Anthology*: "Private Notice", "Living Where You Want To: From the Veterinarian's Journal", "The Going Under of the Evening Land"; *The Chowder Review*: "Asylum"; *Kayak*: "As She Has Been Taught", "Metaphor for the Past"; *The Iowa Review*: "The Will to Live"; *Montana Review*: "The Descent", "Mockingbird", "The Usual Mysteries"; *Poetry East*: "The Delicacy of Freedom"; *Seattle Review*: "The Green Gazebo", "The Sleeping Zebra"; *Tendril*: "Relations", "The Form and Theory of Ordinary Joy", "One River Story", "Walking on This Earth", "The Pain Sweepstakes", "How It Begins", "Loneliness", "Letter to Kathleen in California", "The Waiting Room", "The Arrival of the Unexpected", "Summer", "Ice Fishing", "Marriage".

"A Blessing" and "Over the Phone" originally appeared in *The New Yorker*.

"Aubade", "Or Failing", and "Reversals on a Day that Begins With Rain" originally appeared in *Poetry*.

With special thanks to Charles Simic, James Dalsimer, Jane Shore, Paul Boisvert, Bob and Dolores Russell, David Campbell, Roberta Wood Ealey and Marian Proctor.

The publication of this book is supported by grants from the National Endowment for the Arts in Washington, D.C., a federal agency, and from the Pennsylvania Council on the Arts.

Library of Congress Catalog Number 82-071662
ISBN 0-915605-76-0
ISBN 0-915604-77-9 pbk.
Copyright (c) 1983 by Mekeel McBride

94267

# CONTENTS

"She saw her waist disappear into reflectionless
water; it was like walking into sky, some impurities
of skies. All was one warmth, air, water, and her
own body. All seemed one weight, one matter--
until as she put down her head  and closed her eyes
and the light slipped under her lids, she felt
this matter a translucent one, the river, herself,
the sky all vessels which the sun filled."

-Eudora Welty

"The Wanderers"
*The Golden Apples*

For Peter Petrie


and in memory
of Eric Baker and Connie Holden

*I*

*The Delicacy Of Freedom*

# PRIVATE NOTICE

Now the tigers
hunker and slink
down your quiet street.

They surprise
the neat, narrow gardens
with a generous

ferocity.  They eat roses,
liars, untrue lovers.
Merely to be touched

by the shadow of one
can keep you
sleepless and weeping

with awe. Their eyes,
as hungry as forest fires,
sweep across your clear

window.  The glass does not
ripple or shatter but you
who sleep inside shiver

although this is deep
summer, shiver and begin to dream
that you are loved.

# RELATIONS

*for Charles Simic*

## 1. ABOUT CAUTION

Let's say that whole row of crows on the telephone line
is related.

Let's say seventy different conversations are swept along
in the wire
under their delicate claws.

They are cautious only of wind and questionable weather.
Of human words
they know nothing. They could care less.

In no time at all, they will vanish
into a vise-like horizon,
wise with evening's first clouds.

Caution, caution, little one, is a handkerchief
wet with someone else's tears.

## 2. WHAT THEY WERE LIKE ON THE WIRE

One as auspicious as a thunderstorm.
One with a tin lunch bucket under its wing.
One singing for all the world like a Harvard professor.
One with a piece of turquoise in its beak.
One educated in obituaries.
One not the least bit interested in stars.
One convinced.
One with a strand of yellow hair tucked under its wing.
One with a heart no bigger than a pen-point.
One veering toward celibacy.
One convicted of being infatuated with out-of-the-body travel.
One wanting to cross the road.
One wearing a scarlet eye patch.
One with several onyx-colored wives,
and one, only one, that cannot be described.

# AUBADE

She wakes long before he does.  A fierce shock
of love forces her to look away.  Light
the color of gray silk settles among
the dark fronds of a Phoenix palm.  Asleep
he laughs, as if in whatever world's
now his own, someone dances drunkenly
with an Alaskan bear, or, on a dare
kisses the mayor's bald head, leaving
a perfect red lip print that will amuse
the sparrows for hours.  She watches him sleep
for almost an hour and although he
does not laugh again, nor wake, he talks
a kind of dream-prattle that has in it
parrots and a dove-grey slate still dusty
with the chalk of childhood.  She cannot see
his face buried in the pillow but thinks
how in that pillow he must leave some
residue of dream:  a name, a scar, parts
of a song in which two people now are
dancing.  His red hair flares against
the plain white pillowcase: a benign fire,
rich as any color Rembrandt ever
loved, the first deep whisper of the rising sun.

# THE GREEN GAZEBO

A man and a woman sit in the green gazebo,
the great dream square of park
empty except for a luna moth
which looks, in the distance, as if someone
standing in shadow were waving to them
the pale handkerchief of surrender. And stars
only this once, fleck the inestimable dark
in the way that a first light snowfall
resolves the black meadows of December.
But this is summer.

And they are still sitting in the gazebo.
Grass at the bottom of the wooden stairs
is so wet with dew one might believe
that earlier in the afternoon, a woman
in a yellow dress sat there,
stringing necklaces. And, distracted,
spilled a glittering vial of glass beads
that now catch and magnify
street-lamp light, shining
with the slight patina of displacement.

In the dark gazebo they talk a little and not
softly. Still the cool air carries away
their words and no one hears. They hold
each other, every advantage of imagination
theirs; the loss they face
for now, as far away as the dead stars,
whose intricate light appears to them as beautiful
as tears caught in the eyelashes of the unaware

sleeper. They will have said goodbye
long before morning approaches the empty park.

What can I say of them to keep them
there a little longer? What is there to say?
That they are happpy? That they
are where they ought to be?  How flat that sounds
and stupid, really, when looking
at the two of them, speechless
and together—
the bright grass sweeping in a midnight wind,
a casual and worldly blessing
around the green gazebo.

# OR FAILING

Just before I wake
I am trying
to write this
for you

when someone wearing dusky gloves

holds out
the entire planet
earth, whole

and harvest fat,
some dark
fruit

beaded with sugar, cloud, this weather

as love wills it, warm;
the fruit
newly plucked
from a river

where it had been placed to cool.
All of this

just before waking;
I am
thinking

of you, for a moment

wholly of this
world which is
held out, peculiar

and entire as the astronauts must have
seen it; swathed
in cloud, a ripe and
solitary blue

looking just exactly as if
I might reach out and
hold it or

failing that,
you.

# REVERSALS ON A DAY THAT BEGINS WITH RAIN

### 1.

Outside, the rain is falling
and it has nothing to hold on to.
I have been gone from this room
a long time without you
noticing.

### 2.

Inside, there is an immense wheat field, a red barn,
a horse with a blue bridle.
Everything—anchored by heat,
by harvest. A dragonfly
pins itself to my shoulder, bright reminder
of worlds much smaller than this.
You are in the cool white house, making iced-tea,
slicing great wheels of lemon for the globe-shaped
frosted pitcher.

. . .

### 1.

You turn and take my hand, placing it over your heart
which moves uneasily
like a small, tropical bird, caught.
You ask me: Why is it that crows at dusk
walk the highway's edge as if looking for lost money?

### 2.

You arrive unexpectedly,

the consulate from some country
where everyone, at noon, puts down
packages, laundry, scissors or sorrow
to kiss, move closer to each other,
or perhaps just to look, for a moment
at the hydrangeas, the brown star
of a sparrow settling in among the blossoms.

. . .

1.

I can only talk
when no one is listening.
The room is clean, well-lit. And on the other side,
rain paints itself across the glass,
the pure shellac of loneliness.
I love you. Come back.

2.

This oasis,
with its gardens, its fountains, its cool white rooms
would mean nothing
without the golden ache
of so much sand around us. But anywhere
I would love you just as much.
As for the memory of rain—think of a woman
writing on a steamy window
of some world where it cannot stop,
your name.

# ASYLUM

This is the house where the witch lives—
the house that stands on chicken legs
and spins and spins while the witch inside

spins out the delicate algebra of absence;
today all blue-eyed men will disappear
and tomorrow she will restore them.

She smells of vanilla and the dark forest
of your childhood.  She wears only white

and if you make the mistake of touching her
you will have to dance for the rest of your life
which won't be waltz, which won't be long.

Be careful.  Her red hair is sheer electricity
and more than once she's knocked out all power
in this city, simply by thinking it so.

Her many cats, her flat sad fish, the odd familiars,
love her fiercely but half of this is fear.

When she's cranky with her pretty pets
she turns them, temporarily, into coffee cups
or candles, frying pans or fountain pens,

whatever she thinks she needs at the moment.
Today she thinks she needs to fall in love.
In the quiet asylum of the witch's heart

children are still
making cakes from crushed geraniums and dust.

This is still the day on which all blue-eyed men
have vanished.  And the witch *is* in love.
Look at her eyes shining with thunderstorms!

She is walking everywhere in the world
in her black high-heels.  Where she's walked,
rose bushes, bunches of baby's breath,

small goats and chunks of rough diamonds appear.
She is looking for the man who will not fear her.

She thinks she sees him sleeping
in a white hammock in South Dakota, music
near him like a ghost that knows

it must not leave what it most loved on earth,
an air for flute and continuo.
But then she loses sight of him

as if he, too, were only ghost; as if
there were no other magic in this life besides her own.

# AS SHE HAS BEEN TAUGHT

The building, a tall one, is on fire again.
On the twenty-first floor, she,
dressed in smoky silks,
settles in to watch.
Below, she can see enameled firetrucks
roaring down streets
no wider than the ruler on her desk.

She wonders how they think they'll stop the fire
with their tiny hoses
and matchstick ladders.
Watching her building shadowed on the next
she sees the roof's on fire,
the silhouette of it
fanned into flames

that almost look
like dancers
twining topsy-turvy in a dark field.
She feels safe, feels warm
in the celluloid flames that are,
after all, only the red silks
her sleeping mind has wrapped around her.

But the rescue squad
of volunteer pharmacists,
and paper-pale priests
kicks down the door, helps her
through the iridescent halls
into blackened streets

where she is blanketed
by the ladies auxiliary.

Even though the alarm
has been silenced, they slip her
into the colorless cradle of amnesia
while her lover, his arms scalded
by a great bouquet of crimson roses,
wanders dully
through the water-ruined rooms.

# THE FORM AND THEORY OF ORDINARY JOY

Tonight, there is nothing on this earth I love.

With no difficulty I can say *fuck the weather*
*and fuck the weatherman* in his spotless suit;
his neatly whittled pointer, like a penis he can't
keep in his pants, relentlessly stabbing
at sub-zero temperatures, drought, and pointing out

just how far ash from Mt. St. Helens has drifted
by now

and while I'm on the subject, damn that volcano too,
for being so much less interesting than Pompeii
or the impending disappearance

of California
by earthquake, or the overtake of conservatism,
whichever comes first.

And furthermore, I really dislike the moon,
full as it is; as a matter of fact, because it is full
and, as usual, floating completely out of reach.

No, I no longer love Tutenkauman's ravished gold
nor the high-heeled slippers
on the scented feet of movie stars. Marilyn Monroe,

you can go to hell, along with Einstein,
Offenbach, and Carmen Miranda. And Rilke, you be damned too
for your cheeky insistence on epiphany.

The question then. Better
to be dead? Absolutely not. You slip out

of your body like a woman abandoning
a cheap negligee and first thing
you're met by a militant band
of angels who have been dead god knows how long,

and they hand you roses and apples
and they tell you that it's not going to be as bad as you think,
that being dead

only takes about as much effort
as staying alive.  But they're lying, of course.

They, in their taffetas and kayaks,
move lazily toward what appears to be a picnic
with hams and clams
and French champagne.

But it should be a clue to you, the first of many
when you look closely at the ground,
see red ants,

realize you're looking at small globes
of blood, inching after the bodies that have forsaken them.

# ONE RIVER STORY

When she wakes it will seem possible to mend
the long, uneven scar departure made

on the river.  She lives beside that river;
all night death boats feather down the dark water.

Once in awhile she waves
from the bridge of sleep, the wrought-iron bridge.

Everyone she knows is on those ships
of cloud, those paper boats—

their names scripted in thin calligraphy
on their foreheads or their wrists,

Dennis, Becky, David, Jack.  When they do look
back it is as if to say, *Well at least that is done.*

They pass so quietly she dreams of slipping them
into the live harbor of her shining hand,

her hand that now holds the moon:
a paper lantern, dark flowers printed there.

In the last dream, she is embroidering
on yards and years of water-marked satin

iridescent peaches, nectarines, the sun—
every one of the named and lonely planets, the lost.

# THE DELICACY OF FREEDOM

*for Fred and for P.L.P.*

**1.**
I watch this April morning
as if it were a freshly stretched canvas;
as if Van Gogh,
before he surrenders to the world,
paints with terrible precision,
the paper-cut wings of a crow
against the wind-scoured sky, paints

the unknotting of each bud
until a whole tree pulls up anchor,
drifts lazily away
toward summer.

**2.**
On the way to work, I count
one cat, one raccoon, and a robin,
its orange breast still curiously intact,
dead at the side of the road:

the small deaths
of those lured out into the open
after the military security
of winter.

**3.**
I learn that an acquaintance
five years younger than I

is dying:  cancer.
And an Irishman, now half-blind,
and almost deaf
in his 59th day of starvation
doles out to himself the last
delicacy of freedom
that no Englishman
dares offer him.

I know neither of them
well enough to grieve.
And all along, April continues
to print out
its frilly blossom-gossip
against a topaz sky.

4.
All day my eyes fill up
with tears, like a miser's guarded treasure
from which he lets not even the dullest copper
drop.

Today, it has been so with everyone.

5.
Friend, I see an intricate chandelier
of tear-drop glass
forming at the corner of your eye.  And cannot
reach to brush it
softly into light.
How much easier it would be
to dismiss each tear
as a kind of ice-child, remnant

of the huge
and newly banished winter.

6.
Perhaps it's just that the natural world
fulfills its promises
with an ease beyond us.
The wizened, tough bud
gives way to blossom.
And then the flower
topples from its gentle branch—
a motion that might unbalance a world—
if we knew where to look.

# WALKING ON THIS EARTH

*for Larkin Warren*

A lonely woman
climbs the hill behind her house.  Small
crater at the top:
a bowl,
filled with whatever the moon
has left behind.  At the other end

of the world, in an ordinary vestibule,
summer solstice is being prepared
by two dark men in silks.
They polish the sun's copper surface,
hammer our dents,

lament the storage of other planets
in foreign observatories,
the beauty of them insulted
in the milky lenses
of telescopes, bazookas.  Blue

prints of the stars
now line the cages of parakeets,
the concrete floors of the auto mechanic,

and the silver Tiffany serving dish
of the moon
is eclipsed by a lawyer's
black wig.  Currently,

walking on this earth
is a difficult business.  Still, you've got
in your pockets
a few coins

as silver as the scales
of the Emperor's fighting fish
that you send to roam
the marble basins of old fountains
on errands of wishful thinking

and as for the immaculate clockwork of desire,
it lies strapped to your wrist,
glass moon, halo of black numbers
touched lightly by the hands

of compassion
that pass over them
with astonishing regularity.

# II

## The Waiting Room

for Jim Dalsimer

*"Please, Doctor, I feel a pain.*
*Not here. No, not here. Even I don't know."*

—Czeslaw Milosz
from *Three Talks on Civilization*

# THE PAIN SWEEPSTAKES

is open to all, regardless of age,
opportunity, or interest. Takes no
effort to enroll. When you win, you
win big and we aren't just bragging. Imagine
your cat, flat as a cartoon in the aftermath
of a foreign car; discover your favorite
child feeding on the fine caviar
of barbiturates; find your spouse in bed
with a young student of Russian literature,
whose pink cheeks shine like the Ukranian
dawn. If all else fails we can crack your father's
heart like a walnut left over from last
Christmas, then hook him up to the white heaven
of intensive care. We care about you.
For once, we want you to win.
And the really startling part is how easy
this all is. Keep your hopes high. We draw
your number everytime you sigh at the sad
shape this world is in.

# METAPHOR FOR THE PAST

The sugared, powdered bride stumps
slowly through the white mud of a baker's making.

Her ankle catches in a blue rosette
and when she finally shakes her foot loose,
she loses one oyster-colored shoe.
A curl of her shellaced hair

shakes free, so that already she resembles
a sailor's widow, watching for something
that cannot return.  Hours

later she reaches the edge
of the confectioner's miracle,
but she does not mean to jump and couldn't anyway

half cemented as she is in a beautiful
quicksand of sugar and vanilla.

Below, on the holiday plateau,
she watches children spill champagne;
a golden rain of congratulations
wash over the happy crowd

as now the groom, twenty times her size
appears in white seersucker.

The crowd stands,
cut-glass crystal raised in praise
of continuity, or ritual. Shyly the groom accepts
the heavy silver knife

and moves toward the shining cake,
thinking of how he must cut evenly,

thinking only of the hunger which must
be appeased, the need to keep
the crowd of his inviting loyal, pleased;

the tiny bride on cake-heaven:
a lighthouse in a snow of roses
showing him exactly where to place
the knife's first quiet slice.

# THE BLUE-TEAR POOL

Tears are always blue; save them, fill a swimming
pool. Then throw the baby in. But see! It does not
drown . . . takes out its little grief-napkin, wipes
its eyes, then back-paddles in all of that
salty surplus as if born to it. Next, toss in the dog,
who only asks that you allow it to bring its briefcase of bones. They sink, fleshless treasure, straight
to the heart of the glowing pool. Try it yourself.
Afraid? Of what? Here, the sharks are no bigger than
wisdom teeth. The lifeguard's busy fanning himself
with a pair of lacy underwear. Go ahead. Left foot
first. No danger from the lobsters. They're busy
making love. Or lunching on each other. The water's
warm. The dog's doing high dives so delicate that
one's heart—red egg—almost cracks from the beauty
of it. And baby wants to play. If you give in just
this once, the blue-tear pool will make sure you
float and promises honestly that you'll be allowed
to stay.

# HOW IT BEGINS

Never have you seen anything like it:
the panther wandering from table to table;
azure butterflies drowning
beautifully in the finger bowls;
a lobster on a diamond-studded leash.
Now the cello quartet begins.

The night waiters place fresh flowers
behind your ear, promise that the meat
*will* be rare, the wine
from a fine century previously thought
to be lost. This table is yours.

Be careful how you touch the crystal,
how you talk. Here, things shatter
at sounds beyond whisper.
There are no mirrors, clocks, no mention
ever, of the bill.

Discreetly, the night waiters wheel past you
blindfolded pheasants,
piglets tiny as new roses,
so that you may choose while still alive
what most satisfies.

Relax. Everything is exactly what it seems to be.
The fact that you are dining out alone
should not disturb you. The face now
looming over yours, painted white
and barely breathing, is only here to please.

# LONELINESS

At first the pig is as tiny as a walnut
and so intelligent it answers the phone
taking messages in polite soprano.

She lets it move in, fills its bureau
with acorns, peppermint candies.

Its eyelashes are so long she has to comb them
daily.  The pig grows quickly, pink moon,
never quite full.

It eats the dictionary, a kitchen chair,
her favorite hair brush.  Even so,

she allows for it to stay, saying—
*A simple case of domestic hunger that has its limits.*
The pig continues to eat—

quilts, cooking spoons, the wedding dress
that she has not yet worn.

Eats and eats until it has to eat the living room,
the entire place.  Picture this:  a pig
as big as a five room apartment, grinning . . .

a woman wondering what to do next
when a little door in the pig's side swings open.

It is her dining room she sees inside,
the table neatly set for one, a candle and a rose,
glass platter of uncracked acorns, toy telephone.

# THE DESCENT

*for Manny Cabral*

Rapunzel gets tired of her tower;
the terrible hair that must be combed
daily, and daily lowered as a ladder
to a lover not of her choice, a lover
only too willing to keep her on a level
with clouds and restless sparrows.
When she discovers stairs, she uses them.
In the beauty salon,

scissors are busy clipping out
quick gossip, singing songs adorned
with dollar signs and French perfume.
The lady with the long hair simply says,
*"In this day I do not believe*
*hair should have to do double time*
*or triple as ladder, life and lover."*
Now, new scissors

clip one inch and then another—*Blinded*
*by thorns she planted herself, the witch*
*is dead or dying.  The mortal wound was envy.*
Five inches and then ten—*The opulant*
*prince, now tenant at one narrow*
*stone window, mourns ladders in that high*
*place of cloud and sparrow.*
The lady

with so much weight removed, rises
from the chair, floats just beneath
the ceiling.  She breathes in the rich scent
of red soaps, thick shampoos
that smell of vanilla.  Very nice, she thinks
and then descends in a delight so pure
that even ordinary air is enough
to hold her here.

# LETTER TO KATHLEEN IN CALIFORNIA

That game began when you were five
and I was nine. I'd barricade
the bedroom door
while you solemnly announced
the same rules:
*The floor is hell or death and if you touch it,*
*devil take your soul.*
What were our devils then?
I can't recall but how we leapt about,
safe on the tiny heaven
of furniture surfaces. We named
the blue chair, China; the bureau, Rome;
and twin beds, Bolivia and Brazil,
then swept about the globe
as mindless and free of gravity
as light.

Now your voice, slight on a long distance line,
falters. Your cells, the body's galaxy
begin to swell with the start
of something you can't name out loud.
As you talk,
I sit up in bed, no lights on,
the sheets—
a ghostly tangle at my feet.
Through the thread-thin bars of summer
screen I stare into the dark yard.
There, the fireflies that you loved
on your last visit
blink and bump along, crazy beacons
defying any obstacles that would hinder

their ascent or fall.

Oh, I know better than to call them
stars that have descended
in a kind of blessing.
Unlike stars,
they sweeten only June, July.
Summer after summer, they return,
abdomens swollen with light,
a pulse made visible
that traces illogical, phospher maps
in the frail kingdom
of these ordinary summer nights.
While you live in a place
where the earth can sway, swallow
a woman, a house, then slam shut;
where the rules we made still hold.

Now the phone's back
in its cradle and I keep seeing
the two of us leap from surface
to surface, into a heaven
of our own design
and all the while
beneath us
the world shines with sentinel trees;
blue rope, gray thread of river and road
unravelling into an empty field;
telegraph of grass
blade to blade, waving
silently over the earth, this
earth that finally will pull us down.

# THE WAITING ROOM

A waterfall, late autumn, practices
the flimsy, overused art of escape.
This tumble of summer-drained lake
is no more than disloyal silk, cascading
from the magician's black sleeve.
No salmon leap here, no single leaf
stays still enough to print
its copper-colored star on water skin.
The journey's swift; a stick, a paper boat,
one pale gold crysanthemum sweep past
the solemn, lamp-bright windows of a woman
who is knitting a blanket of black wool
that spills from her lap onto the floor
like the huge flag of an army
that knows the odds of its winning
but begins slowly and with grace
to prepare for battle anyway.

# THE ARRIVAL OF THE UNEXPECTED

You are driving home in a country
that is both lovely and familiar.  The fields
mowed for the last time before snow
can harbor now
nothing wild.  Mice sleep in spools and sacs of air
among the fragile roots
of crops long harvested.  Attending trees
stand as calm and kind as parlor lamps
while darkness, almost gently, rises
up among them.

You are lost only
in the thought of how far away summer has become,
your own tiredness,
the tranquility of the field . . .
when suddenly a red buck rises up,
an antlered buck, three hundred pounds
or more, making of himself and you—
through some awful symmetry—
a convergence of volition, force, and density.
Quickly he becomes the final destination
you could never have predicted for yourself.

He leaps desperately toward the spot
where the two of you will connect,
so single-minded as to misunderstand
your presence, or worse, dismiss it.
Your only thought is to keep
from harming him
although this is as impossible
as the appearance of an angel
or the absence of all sorrow in this world.
You pull hard on the wheel,
slam down the brake.

*No* is the one word you say aloud

as if now, with everything out of control, a single word
could keep you safe.  The car tips.  Slow
motion, about to leap, the buck turns,
looks straight at you.  Time,
not only slow, but stopped.  You catch in his eye
an odd glance, shared glimpse
acknowledging death between you
no thicker than a needle.
Then, with heart-stopping grace, the two of you
veer apart, never having touched.

The car, obedient now only to itself, rocks
and spins and finally settles in the wrong lane.
You are left shaking,
the buck now absent, no evidence
to show how you got to where you are.
Later, home, there is a letter from a friend
who writes to say he hopes that all is well;
that the weather has remained mild;
the trees celebratory in their change of color;
mostly he hopes that you are happy.

As you set aside the envelope
you realize how close that message came
to never reaching you; know the beauty of facing
it at such close range without harm;
the alarming largeness your life
has taken on.  Then, quite without reason,
you feel the joy of an incurable
suddenly healed
as you think again of the buck—
much larger than any earthly animal—
disappearing into the dark and snowless field.

# MOCKINGBIRD

The mockingbird's a live encyclopedia
of song.  Listen, it can be
the whole world humming to itself:
tinsel consonant of wind
in love with whatever its silken glove
touches, never touches

and then again its just the normal chatter
of thrush or grackle.
The mockingbird's own song?  Difficult
to hear in this aria that includes
news from every absent bird,
but slightly richer.  All night

it stays awake, slipping its glad opera
into the delicate bone cage
of the Emperor's or your sleeping
ear.  For this, the glass-blower wakes
and weeps, knowing how frail his world is
and imperfect.

# SUMMER

A butterfly lights
on the eyelid
of a woman
sleeping
in the sun.
Light passes through
the stained glass
window
of one wing:
her cheek
as blue as if
berries had been
crushed there.

# THE GOING UNDER OF THE EVENING LAND

*"But it should be quite a sight,*
*the going under of the evening land . . .*
*And I can tell you, my young friend,*
*it is evening.  It is very late."*

—Walker Percy
*The Moviegoer*


In the evening land, a woman
places fresh bread on a polished table.
She turns on lamps, watching light
make golden maps on table top and parquet floor.
Here, without her knowing,
an interior continent completes itself.
She listens

to the glittery chatter of silverware
released from drawers that smell of Chinese tea.
Crows begin sleep now,
a few stars hidden in their pockets of black silk.
In the evening land
she considers how darkness leans cleanly
into its bright double—

how neither leaves for very long.  Outside,
a child plays hide and seek with the rose bush
ghost.  Now between light and dark,
the world splits open but only a little—

what is, what could be.  And in this time
there are words that no one needs to speak:
                              I woke last night

thinking the bed to be an ocean liner
in touch with Antarctica, something
breaking up, something going under.
Tier on tier, the glittery necklace of the ship
sinking, or the iceberg singing, but I was
safe, I was safe and I
wanted you to know.

# III.

## Living Where You Want To

# ON THE NATURE OF AUTOBIOGRAPHY
# OR AN ADMISSION OF CONCERN

Those of you who can't sleep, this is for you.

For you, who were born in Detroit and even now
lie dreaming of wrenches and pulleys
and shit in the alleys
where your children have to play.

For the heart attack victim who survives but who cannot
keep a clock in his house,
for fear it will stop.

For the divorced woman
with nine clocks or more, each one telling
a slightly different story.

And you, whose wife just died, who must go home
every night to a house immense in its emptiness.

Let's not mince words.  Let's not even call this
a poem.  There's nothing that pretty left in the world,
nothing of value that audible.

And so this is for you, who, after the abortion,
see squirrels or oppossums or dogs
in your night headlights, swerve, lose
control, sit sweating at the side of the road
over what was, after all, imaginary.

And the men with no jobs who drink
their wive's cheap perfume for its scarce alcohol,

and would, but cannot, howl wholesome with some
half rising moon.

This is for those of you—wing-walker, banker,
or priest, who believe love
exists but are too terrified to attempt it.

For students who love the words *hope* and *soul* and *truth*
unable to define them in terms that touch
their own lives and so shelter themselves in the abstract,
a tact the Detroit men would envy.

Most of all, for the ones who dislike poetry
and would see, even in this,
some secret kept against them. There's little more to be said.

Just that some people love words
as much as a locksmith loves the machine
that duplicates keys, allowing the lost
to once again enter familiar rooms,

touch the chipped blue china cup,
stand quietly in the sun-glazed kitchen,
amazed that such return, in this world, is possible.

# MORNING

Morning is not so distant
from the windows in this house
where a woman is happy.

Certainly, she wakes for awhile
in the dark
and then sleeps again
face pressed into shadow,

looking down, as if in sleep
to see the root
of the matter. The roots rock and hum
in their ancient understanding

of something as simple
as earth pressed close.
Something pressed close;

the house, the land
it stands on
all rocked in the pale blue palm
of dawn.

# ICE FISHING

*for Ian MacKenzie*

You're out on the ice again,
today warmer
than the weatherman has made
allowance for,

so you test each step, wondering
if the weight
of one solitary man can stand
on this
endless glass plateau.

Still early, you sit gazing
into opaque water,
the tackle box untouched.
Your vision fills
not with the expected

swift glitter of fish
but instead
a woman,
February light

lying across the taut
strings of a violin
that she has just placed
on her lap;
the elegance of all things,

like the Brahms
she has played a part of,
famished both for silence
and for the beginning note again.

You want to let yourself slip
into unfathomable descent
to find just exactly where
she lies—
flawless statuary,

swathed in the black silk
of moving water, of memory.
Instead, you unpack
the silver hooks,
meaning to bait them

but they catch
in your hand the sun's rising light
so that it looks
for a second as if your black glove
is burning,

as if you, faithful and with no knowledge
of consequence, have brought
for the first time
the secret of warmth
to an early world.

Suddenly happy, you scatter the hooks
across the ice.  It is enough,
for now, to let the deep region
keep its sleepy harvest
of blind swimmers, enough

to watch in the uncomplicated sky,
the sun, still so close
you might pull it
like an orange

into your palm
and suck the sweet juice out,
while all around your feet
the fallen hooks
shine like small question marks.

# THE SLEEPING ZEBRA

*for Manny Cabral*

In your kitchen, beside the long white table,
plants touch all the way
to ceiling from the floor.

This is the private war against winter:
tropical, a pot of growing daffodils,
each stem with dancer's posture,
each flower, seasoned lantern.

We will sit for hours with no
special need to talk.  But when I change chairs
I see, under the *while* and *if* of an ordinary life,

under the table,
the porcelain figure of a sleeping zebra,
no bigger than a real cat, its gentle head

curved away in some dream impossible to guess.
Oh!  but we let it be
with only a casual remark or two:

*It was a gift*, you say. *I'd never buy one*
*for myself.*
Myself?  I'd want a thin red leash to lead the secret
creature from room to quiet room.  But our talk
turns to home heating, food's rising cost,
and then it's time for me to leave.
Deep in the world and later, there's still

the plain black and white
of what is always here.  Neither convict's mark
not simple riddle, the zebra rises,

breathes gently on my sleeping face
or yours.  Its hooves on linoleum, on polished wood
do not wake us

like the small hail
of ordinary weather at the window,
more like

pearl after pearl being dropped
in a porcelain box,
not one lost, nothing lost.

# LIVING WHERE YOU WANT TO: FROM THE VETERINARIAN'S JOURNAL

*for Jack Titolo*

Have seen my last human being.
As I recall, a woman with macaw.
Ailment?  She says the bird won't talk.

Tied tongue.  I try to tell her
that no cure for that can be called cure.
Before she has a chance to listen

the macaw sweeps its wings wide open
as if somewhere there is a silent orchestra
waiting for just such signs;

a sunrise poised, a playful
wind that wants the roof erased.
Without reason, then

the lady suddenly assumes the shape
of a tropical palm, and what was the cage
lies in its shade, an old guitar.

It was not, after all, difficult
or unexpected.  I lean into equator heat,
eat guavas, listen to the blue telegraph

of jeweled insects
that sting the air with sweetness
beyond words.

The next patient—a tortoise-shell cat
sweeps her shy, silk shadow
the length of this midwestern porch.

I sit in white wicker.
Cat purrs, throat full of bells,
curls into a perfect circle.

Sunflowers heavy with sleep
the cat and I will share
lean closer, close.

And on Thursdays, the Newfoundland dog
that any novice hunter in New Hampshire
would shoot as bear

brings October with her and a river,
forest half gone to gold, no guns.
Dog lies half submerged—black lily,

eating apples that I toss, or chocolate.
Cured into quiet ecstasy, I watch
a creature far too small to name

pattern out one odd star on water-skin.
Since then, I have lived this way, surrounded
by whatever country the animals bring in.

# THE USUAL MYSTERIES

White fence keeps the shy
sunflower in; keeps me close
to the cool, blue telephone
of a morning glory.  No one's here
but the dappled cat

quite contained in sleep
that drowsy sun doles out
deliciously without coast
or ocean, any named or known
geography.  It's May;

I paint the fence again and think
on how it never can keep out
real harm:  the hunger of what lives
underground, the sky's selfish
need for storm.

Afternoon, and the cat
disappears through two paint-wet pickets.
She slips
out of present tense,
tips away from easy

harvest.  With ballet-grace,
with no regret,
she's pulled ahead by the invisible
string of her singular hunger,
stalking what is just out of reach.  Now,

without malice, dusk.
As light dissolves
so does the fence. A sparrow sinks
into its nest of dust.
Dust thickens in the dark blue throat

of the morning glory; everything is going
away and still the message
is not clear, except that each
year the stars are brighter
than they ever were before

and evening is generous
with its gifts—this orange
for an instant, swollen with what it has
sung up from sweet dark
and difficult sun

alike. The usual
mysteries are everywhere, only now
more visible. What
I desire to capture or to
love, I will become.

# POETRY

Once in a blue moon, the bait's
set correctly and cactus
blooms.  Hours of work.  And of course,

the jackhammer man goes home hurting,
for which he is paid
handsomely.  He has an hourglass
heart, a tiny thimble

wife who willingly sets a plate
of calm beets before him and lamb.
Romance is no longer at stake.

They would not think
to eat by candle light,
the jackhammer man and his tidy wife.
Who needs a life

in which the pork is as pink
as a hybrid rose, the cauliflower,
a knoll of Austrian snow?  Outside,

the lawn is lighted by statues
of past presidents.
Beyond what slight light they cast

a woman in a blue hood wanders.
In her basket:
blood oranges from Spain, musky truffles,
velvet mushrooms from the Baltic shore.


They will ignore her for as long
as they stay awake but in sleep

the jackhammer man keeps his hand
on his wife's small breast

kneading it like the snowy dough
he remembers from childhood
when he looked in the baker's window

at the tall man
in the confectionary hat, who sang,
as all around him
the newly formed loaves began to rise.

# THE PHARMACIST GOES CLOUD BATHING

**1.**
Cloud bathing is illegal
in Massachusetts.
This does not concern the pharmacist
whose white coat
can attract even the most distant
cirrus formation.  Happy the man
who does not feel the need
to hasten the invisible!

**2.**
Birds understand, rise
in time on wings that weigh far less
than bodies,
live sometimes for days in the opulent hotel
of heat-inflated August clouds.

**3.**
He carries a briefcase most customers never see.
Inside, a sketchbook for secret
explorations of the cloud—
its sumptuous architecture,
its tenuous hold on the material,
its terrible need to descend
to a human level.

**4.**
His reasons?
He will reveal only that his skin's sensitive.
He sees something in this
anyone else would classify invisible.
Medicine?  Certainly, he says spilling

vitamin C tablets on the counter.
These are the citrus children of a cloud
that once came down for brief romance
and discovered how it feels to have a body.

5.

But the pharmacist's out on Massachusetts Avenue
opening his white towel.
Neon sign for the store
although only inches away
eases into mist, appears and disappears
like a tropical bird
mysteriously caught in a blizzard.

6.

Spread out beside him on the towel—
things that might seduce a cloud:
pearl necklaces that once belonged
to Billie Holliday,
a thick bundle of hot-house lilies,
small clay birds with rosy throats.

7.

The pharmacist's entirely undressed in public!
but you can't see.
He turns on a tiny radio that reports
inclement weather
then switches to a young girl
playing a mandolin in Tennessee.
The cloud bather falls asleep
in the huge room
of a heavenly body where he dreams

oranges, a certain red-haired girl from childhood,
white chickens at dusk.

8.
When he's had enough
he resumes his normal occupation.
Above him now
clouds disperse and sleep
invisible in their true homes:
the white eye of zero,
paint sets and milk bottles,
the calm tops of Panama hats
and the confection of uncut wedding cakes.
Loving anything,
the cloud bather will tell you,
makes it enough.

# THE WILL TO LIVE

On the green lawn of a city park
a sentence of dark insects completes itself:

Believe!  Believe!
Above, two Monarchs matter and flash

in this immense summer air.
Small scraps of wing, good weather, a will

to live, they come
from the tenuous country of now

whatever the heart is asking for.  Even if I
weren't here

they'd still congratulate the sky
with a fragile disbelief in sorrow.  Graceful

as the hands of the deaf
they form a language in air that I understand

almost not at all.  Being human
I might say

they kiss and part and kiss again, but
know they're governed by desire

or law or lack of these
beyond me.  They fling themselves

against a sky so big
they do not understand it's there.  Clouds

fat and ample, grow
fatter still and if the old June maples

stand weighted and without words
it is not from human grief, or any other.

# CARNEGIE-MELLON POETRY

**1975**
*The Living and the Dead*, Ann Hayes
*In the Face of Descent*, T. Alan Broughton

**1976**
*The Week the Dirigible Came*, Jay Meek
*Full of Lust and Good Usage*, Stephen Dunn

**1977**
*How I Escaped from the Labyrinth and
    Other Poems*, Philip Dacey
*The Lady from the Dark Green Hills*, Jim Hall
*For Luck: Poems 1962-1977*, H.L. Van Brunt
*By the Wreckmaster's Cottage*, Paula Rankin

**1978**
*New & Selected Poems*, James Bertolino
*A Circus of Needs*, Stephen Dunn
*The Sun Fetcher*, Michael Dennis Browne
*The Crowd Inside*, Elizabeth Libbey

**1979**
*Paying Back the Sea*, Philip Dow
*Swimmer in the Rain*, Robert Wallace
*Far From Home*, T. Alan Broughton
*The Room Where Summer Ends*, Peter Cooley
*No Ordinary World*, Mekeel McBride

**1980**
*And the Man Who Was Traveling
    Never Got Home*, H.L. Van Brunt
*Drawing on the Walls*, Jay Meek
*The Yellow House on the Corner*, Rita Dove
*The 8-Step Grapevine*, Dara Wier
*The Mating Reflex*, Jim Hall

**1981**
*A Little Faith,* John Skoyles
*Augers,* Paula Rankin
*Walking Home from the Icehouse,* Vern Rutsala
*Work and Love,* Stephen Dunn
*The Rote Walker,* Mark Jarman
*Morocco Journal,* Richard Harteis
*Songs of a Returning Soul,* Elizabeth Libbey

**1982**
*The Granary,* Kim R. Stafford
*Calling the Dead,* C.G. Hanzlicek
*Dreams Before Sleep,* T. Alan Broughton
*Sorting It Out,* Anne S. Perlman
*Love is Not a Consolation;*
   *It is a Light,* Primus St. John

**1983**
*The Going Under of the Evening*
   *Land,* Mekeel McBride
*Museum,* Rita Dove
*Nightseasons,* Peter Cooley

# A BLESSING

*"Freely chosen, discipline
is absolute freedom."*
-Ron Serino


1.
The blue shadow of dawn settles
its awkward silks into the enamelled kitchen
and soon you will wake with me into the long
discipline of light and day—the morning sky
startled and starred with returning birds.
You half-whisper, half-sigh, "This will never stop."
And I say, "Look at the constellations
our keys and coins make, there,
on the polished sky of the dresser top."

2.
From what sometimes seems an arbitrary
form or discipline often come two words
that rhyme and in the rhyming fully marry
the world of spoons and sheets and common birds
to another world that we have always known
where the waterfall of dawn does not drown
even the haloed gnat; where we are shown
how to find and hold the pale day moon, round
and blessed in the silver lake of a coffee spoon.

# OVER THE PHONE

This is where he finds you. February. Over the phone
his voice has in it:  plum tree, pear, a meadow.
Let's say that what he speaks

is an awakening, very early, no alarm.
In each room, you, astonished, find vases, cups and jars
vivid with white heather,

hepatica, great golden daffodils!  Wonder
if you have to, who has the extra key,
who walked the house while you lay sleeping, how high

the price will be for this profusion
from the florist's heart; here, every container's filled
to overflowing and you, though unaware, owe

nothing. Simply notice heliotrope
spilling from the open oven—a sweet, blue bread;
the evening scent of honeysuckle

swelling from a yellow kettle—tea, long summer-steeped.
This is still winter, the door
still swollen with cold and difficult to open.

Even so, see how easily that one dizzy tiger lily
lifts from the heart of the keyhole,
shaped like a Tiffany lamp and shining.

# MARRIAGE

In our yard at night:
the patternless, scatterings of light
from phospher-bellied glow worms,
and presences barely awake
in a slender wine-glass elm.

By day, twelve sets of windchimes
make glassy chatter on front
porch and back.  And hanging from the oak
magazine rack, a page—open
to an x-rayed nautilus—

so that we can see how the creature
moved forward at steady intervals
sealing, for buoyancy,
the chambers it had outgrown,
proving both loss and beauty
to be of use.

In the kitchen, my face and yours
shine from a new copper kettle.
The glitter distorts us slightly
but still, we look benevolent and shy
as if unaccustomed to this

shared reflection.  An operatic release
of steam signals time to settle
at the wooden table where we

are still too careful
with the hand-blown goblets.

A stem, thin as the leg of a heron,
holds up the dark cup
in which flecks of Andromeda
lie sealed, safe in the night-sky glass.
But as we touch

them to each other, they do not crack;
one click, the note caught
in a whip-poor-will's throat.  We drink.
And years pass.

# CARNEGIE-MELLON POETRY

**1975**
*The Living and the Dead*, Ann Hayes
*In the Face of Descent*, T. Alan Broughton

**1976**
*The Week the Dirigible Came*, Jay Meek
*Full of Lust and Good Usage*, Stephen Dunn

**1977**
*How I Escaped from the Labyrinth and
    Other Poems*, Philip Dacey
*The Lady from the Dark Green Hills*, Jim Hall
*For Luck: Poems 1962-1977*, H.L. Van Brunt
*By the Wreckmaster's Cottage*, Paula Rankin

**1978**
*New & Selected Poems*, James Bertolino
*A Circus of Needs*, Stephen Dunn
*The Sun Fetcher*, Michael Dennis Browne
*The Crowd Inside*, Elizabeth Libbey

**1979**
*Paying Back the Sea*, Philip Dow
*Swimmer in the Rain*, Robert Wallace
*Far From Home*, T. Alan Broughton
*The Room Where Summer Ends*, Peter Cooley
*No Ordinary World*, Mekeel McBride

**1980**
*And the Man Who Was Traveling
    Never Got Home*, H.L. Van Brunt
*Drawing on the Walls*, Jay Meek
*The Yellow House on the Corner*, Rita Dove
*The 8-Step Grapevine*, Dara Wier
*The Mating Reflex*, Jim Hall

**1981**

*A Little Faith*, John Skoyles
*Augers*, Paula Rankin
*Walking Home from the Icehouse*, Vern Rutsala
*Work and Love*, Stephen Dunn
*The Rote Walker*, Mark Jarman
*Morocco Journal*, Richard Harteis
*Songs of a Returning Soul*, Elizabeth Libbey

**1982**

*The Granary*, Kim R. Stafford
*Calling the Dead*, C.G. Hanzlicek
*Dreams Before Sleep*, T. Alan Broughton
*Sorting It Out*, Anne S. Perlman
*Love is Not a Consolation;*
    *It is a Light*, Primus St. John

**1983**

*The Going Under of the Evening*
    *Land*, Mekeel McBride
*Museum*, Rita Dove
*Nightseasons*, Peter Cooley